W9-AKU-074

# INTEGRATING
# Growth OF A Nation
## with Reading Instruction

**6 Complete Social Studies Units**

## Written by
Trisha Callella

**Editor:** LaDawn Walter
**Illustrator:** Jenny Campbell
**Cover Illustrator:** Rick Grayson
**Designer/Production:** Moonhee Pak/ Carrie Carter
**Cover Designer:** Moonhee Pak
**Art Director:** Tom Cochrane
**Project Director:** Carolea Williams

# Table of Contents

# Introduction

For many students, reading comprehension diminishes when they read nonfiction text. Students often have difficulty understanding social studies vocabulary, making inferences, and grasping social studies concepts. With so much curriculum to cover each day, social studies content is sometimes put on the back burner when it comes to academic priorities. *Integrating Growth of a Nation with Reading Instruction* provides the perfect integration of social studies content with specific reading instruction to help students improve their comprehension of nonfiction text and maximize every minute of your teaching day.

This resource includes six units that relate to the establishment and expansion of America. The units are based on the most common social studies topics taught in grades 3–4 in accordance with the national social studies standards:

**Native Americans**　　　　**Branches of Government**
**Spanish Missions in America**　**Historical Documents**
**The Gold Rush**　　　　　**Citizenship**

Each unit includes powerful prereading strategies, such as predicting what the story will be about, accessing prior knowledge, and brainstorming about vocabulary that may be included in the reading selection. Following the prereading exercises is a nonfiction reading selection written on a grade 3–4 reading level. Each reading selection is followed by essential postreading activities such as comprehension questions on multiple taxonomy levels, skill reviews, and a critical thinking exercise. Each unit also includes a hands-on activity that connects each social studies topic to students' lives. The descriptions on pages 5–8 include the objectives and implementation strategies for each unit component.

Before, during, and after reading the story, students are exposed to the same reading strategies you typically reinforce during your language arts instruction block and guided reading. This powerful duo gives you the opportunity to teach both reading and social studies simultaneously. Using the activities in this resource, students will continue *learning to read* while *reading to learn*. They will become more successful readers while gaining new social studies knowledge and experiences.

**Prereading Strategies**

✓ Catch a Clue
✓ Concept Map
✓ Word Warm-Up

**Nonfiction Text**

**Postreading Applications**

✓ Comprehension Questions
✓ Sharpen Your Skills
✓ Get Logical

**Hands-on Social Studies**

# Connections to Standards

This chart shows the concepts that are covered in each unit based on the national social studies standards.

| | Native Americans | Spanish Missions in America | The Gold Rush | Branches of Government | Historical Documents | Citizenship |
|---|---|---|---|---|---|---|
| Gain an understanding of how experiences may be interpreted differently by different groups of people. | ● | ● | ● | | | ● |
| Compare ways people from different cultures think about and deal with their physical environment and social conditions. | ● | ● | | | | ● |
| Gain an understanding of cultural unity and diversity within and across groups. | ● | ● | | | | ● |
| Gain an understanding of group influences such as religious beliefs, laws, and peer pressure on people, events, and elements of culture. | | ● | | | | |
| Describe the American Indian nations in various regions and how they adapted to their natural environments. | ● | | | | | |
| Compare and contrast differences about past events, people, places, or situations, and identify how they contribute to our understanding of the past. | ● | ● | ● | ● | ● | ● |
| Identify rights and responsibilities of citizens. | | | | | | ● |
| Identify American symbols, landmarks, and essential historical documents. | | | | | ● | |
| Understand the role of rules and laws in our daily lives and the basic structure of the U.S. government. | | | | ● | | |

# Unit Overview

## Catch a Clue

Objectives

Students will

✓ be introduced to key concepts and vocabulary *before* reading

✓ be able to transfer this key strategy to improve test-taking skills

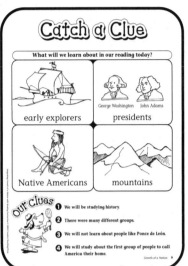

Implementation

Students will use clues and the process of elimination to predict what the nonfiction reading selection will be about. Copy this page on an overhead transparency, and use it for a whole-class activity. Begin by reading aloud each word, and ask students to repeat the words. Read the clues one at a time. Then, discuss with the class what topic(s) could be eliminated and the reasons why. (Note: There will be clues that do not eliminate any topics. The purpose of this is to teach students that although there is information listed, it is not always helpful information.) Cross off a topic when the class decides that it does not fit the clues. If there is more than one topic left after the class discusses all of the clues, this becomes a prediction activity. When this occurs, reread the clues with the class, and discuss which answer would be most appropriate given the clues provided.

## Concept Map

Objectives

Students will

✓ access prior knowledge by brainstorming what they already know about the topic

✓ increase familiarity with the social studies content by hearing others' prior knowledge experiences

✓ revisit the map *after* reading to recall information from the reading selection

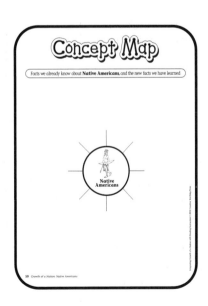

Implementation

Copy this page on an overhead transparency, and use it for a whole-class activity. Use a colored pen to write students' prior knowledge on the transparency. After the class reads the story, use a different colored pen to add what students learned.

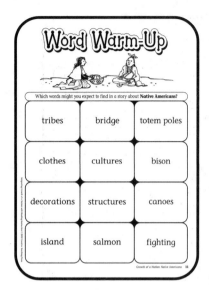

# Word Warm-Up

## Objectives

Students will

✓ be introduced to new vocabulary words

✓ make predictions about the story using thinking and reasoning skills

✓ begin to monitor their own comprehension

## Implementation

Students will use the strategy of exclusion brainstorming to identify which words are likely to be in the story and which words are unrelated and should be eliminated from the list. Copy this page on an overhead transparency, and use it for a whole-class activity. Have students make predictions about which of the vocabulary words could be in the story and which words probably would not be in the story. Ask them to give reasons for their predictions. For example, say *Do you think decorations would be in a story about Native Americans?* A student may say *Yes, because Native Americans decorated totem poles and their homes* or *No, because decorations are only for parties.* Circle the word if a student says that it will be in the story, and cross it out if a student says it will not be in the story. Do not correct students' responses. After reading, students can either confirm or disconfirm their own predictions. It is more powerful for students to verify their predictions on their own than to be told the answer before ever reading the story.

## Nonfiction Text

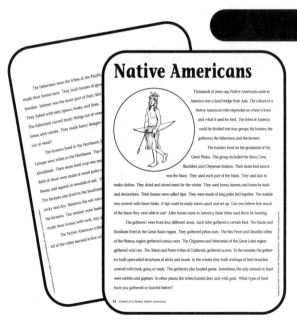

# The Story

## Objectives

Students will

✓ read high-interest, nonfiction stories

✓ increase social studies knowledge

✓ increase content area vocabulary

✓ make connections between social studies facts and their own experiences

## Implementation

Give each student a copy of the story, and display the corresponding Word Warm-Up transparency while you read the story with the class. After the class reads the story, go back to the transparency, and have students discuss their predictions in relation to the new information they learned in the story. Invite students to identify any changes they would make on the transparency and give reasons for their responses. Then, revisit the corresponding Concept Map transparency, and write the new information students have learned.

# Postreading Applications

## Comprehension Questions

### Objectives

Students will

✓ recall factual information

✓ be challenged to think beyond the story facts to make inferences

✓ connect the story to other reading, their own lives, and the world around them

### Implementation

Use these questions to facilitate a class discussion of the story. Choose the number and types of questions that best meet the abilities of your class.

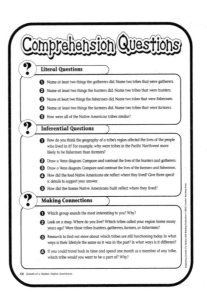

## Sharpen Your Skills

### Objectives

Students will

✓ practice answering questions in common test-taking formats

✓ integrate language arts skills with social studies knowledge

### Implementation

After the class reads a story, give each student a copy of this page. Ask students to read each question and all of the answer choices for that question before deciding on an answer. Show them how to use their pencil to completely fill in the circle for their answer. Invite students to raise their hand if they have difficulty reading a question and/or the answer choices. Thoroughly explain the types of questions and exactly what is being asked the first few times students use this reproducible.

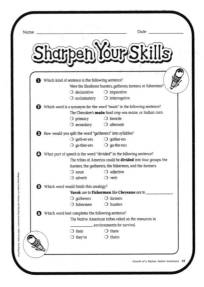

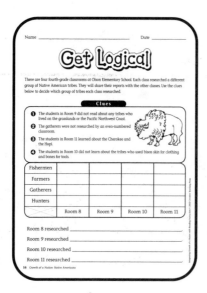

# Get Logical

## Objectives

Students will

✓ practice logical and strategic thinking skills

✓ practice the skill of process of elimination

✓ transfer the information read by applying it to new situations

## Implementation

Give each student a copy of this page. Read the beginning sentences and the clues to familiarize students with the words. Show students step-by-step how to eliminate choices based on the clues given. Have students place an X in a box that represents an impossible choice, thereby narrowing down the options for accurate choices. Once students understand the concept, they can work independently on this reproducible.

# Hands-on Social Studies

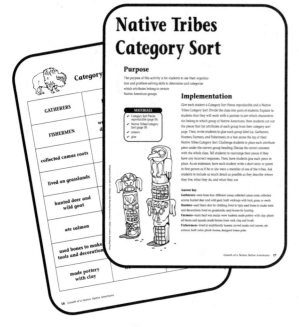

# Social Studies Activity

## Objectives

Students will

✓ participate in hands-on learning experiences

✓ expand and reinforce social studies knowledge

✓ apply new social studies vocabulary words

## Implementation

The social studies activities in this book incorporate a variety of skills students are required to experience at this age level (e.g., survey, interview, analyze, evaluate). Each hands-on activity begins with an explanation of its purpose to help direct the intended learning. Give each student a copy of any corresponding reproducibles and/or materials for the activity. Then, introduce the activity and explain the directions. Model any directions that may be difficult for students to follow on their own.

# Catch a Clue

**What will we learn about in our reading today?**

early explorers

George Washington    John Adams

presidents

Native Americans

mountains

**Our Clues**

**1** We will be studying history.

**2** There were many different groups.

**3** We will not learn about people like Ponce de León.

**4** We will study about the first group of people to call America their home.

# Concept Map

Facts we already know about **Native Americans,** and the new facts we have learned

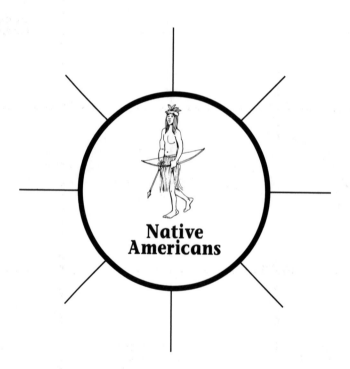

Native
Americans

*Integrating Growth of a Nation with Reading Instruction* © 2002 Creative Teaching Press

# Word Warm-Up

Which words might you expect to find in a story about **Native Americans?**

| | | |
|---|---|---|
| tribes | bridge | totem poles |
| clothes | cultures | bison |
| decorations | structures | canoes |
| island | salmon | fighting |

Integrating Growth of a Nation with Reading Instruction © 2002 Creative Teaching Press

# Native Americans

Thousands of years ago, Native Americans came to America over a land bridge from Asia. The culture of a Native American tribe depended on where it lived and what it used for food. The tribes of America could be divided into four groups: the hunters, the gatherers, the fishermen, and the farmers.

The hunters lived on the grasslands of the Great Plains. This group included the Sioux, Crow, Blackfeet, and Cheyenne Indians. Their main food source was the bison. They used each part of the bison. They used skin to make clothes. They dried and stored meat for the winter. They used horns, hooves, and bones for tools and decorations. Their homes were called tipis. They were made of long poles tied together. The outside was covered with bison hides. A tipi could be easily taken apart and set up. Can you believe how much of the bison they were able to use? After horses came to America, these tribes used them for hunting.

The gatherers were from four different areas. Each tribe gathered a certain food. The Paiute and Shoshone lived in the Great Basin region. They gathered piñon nuts. The Nez Percé and Umatilla tribes of the Plateau region gathered camas roots. The Chippewa and Menomini of the Great Lakes region gathered wild rice. The Yokut and Pomo tribes of California gathered acorns. In the summer, the gatherers built open-sided structures of sticks and brush. In the winter, they built wickiups of bent branches covered with bark, grass, or reeds. The gatherers also hunted game. Sometimes, the only animals to hunt were rabbits and gophers. In other places, the tribes hunted deer and wild goat. What types of food have you gathered or hunted before?

*Integrating Growth of a Nation with Reading Instruction © 2002 Creative Teaching Press*

The fishermen were the tribes of the Pacific Northwest Coast. The Tlingit, Haida, and Yurok made their homes here. They built houses of spruce and cedar planks. These houses held many families. Salmon was the main part of their diet. The fishermen built fishing platforms over a river. They fished with nets, spears, hooks, and lines. They smoked the salmon and stored it for winter. The fishermen carved many things out of wood. They designed totem poles and carved masks, boxes, and canoes. They made fancy designs on all of these items. Have you ever carved omething out of wood?

The farmers lived in the Northeast, Southeast, and Southwest. The Iroquois and the Lenni-Lenape were tribes in the Northeast. The Cherokee, Creek, and Chicksaw were tribes in the sSoutheast. Their main food crop was maize, or Indian corn. They lived in wigwams and longhouses. Both of these were made of wood poles covered with bark or grass mats. The women planted maize, beans, and squash in mounds of soil. The men used bows and arrows to hunt deer, bear, and fox. The farmers also lived in the Southwest. The Hopi and Zuni tribes lived there. Their land was very rocky and dry. However, the soil was good for planting if there was enough water. Here, the men were the farmers. The women wove baskets and made pottery with clay. The farmers of the Southwest made their homes with rock, clay, and brush. What is your home made of?

The Native American tribes had different ways of life. However, they had one thing in common. All of the tribes learned to live with the land. They learned to use what was available in their region.

# Comprehension Questions

##  Literal Questions

**1** Name at least two things the gatherers did. Name two tribes that were gatherers.

**2** Name at least two things the hunters did. Name two tribes that were hunters.

**3** Name at least two things the fishermen did. Name two tribes that were fishermen.

**4** Name at least two things the farmers did. Name two tribes that were farmers.

**5** How were all of the Native American tribes similar?

## Inferential Questions

**1** How do you think the geography of a tribe's region affected the lives of the people who lived in it? For example, why were tribes in the Pacific Northwest more likely to be fishermen than farmers?

**2** Draw a Venn diagram. Compare and contrast the lives of the hunters and gatherers.

**3** Draw a Venn diagram. Compare and contrast the lives of the farmers and fishermen.

**4** How did the food Native Americans ate reflect where they lived? Give three specific details to support your answer.

**5** How did the homes Native Americans built reflect where they lived?

##  Making Connections

**1** Which group sounds the most interesting to you? Why?

**2** Look on a map. Where do you live? Which tribes called your region home many years ago? Were those tribes hunters, gatherers, farmers, or fishermen?

**3** Research to find out more about which tribes are still functioning today. In what ways is their lifestyle the same as it was in the past? In what ways is it different?

**4** If you could travel back in time and spend one month as a member of any tribe, which tribe would you want to be a part of? Why?

*Integrating Growth of a Nation with Reading Instruction © 2002 Creative Teaching Press*

# Sharpen Your Skills

**1** Which kind of sentence is the following sentence?

Were the Shoshone hunters, gatherers, farmers, or fishermen?
- ○ declarative
- ○ imperative
- ○ exclamatory
- ○ interrogative

**2** Which word is a synonym for the word "main" in the following sentence?

The Cherokee's **main** food crop was maize, or Indian corn.
- ○ primary
- ○ favorite
- ○ secondary
- ○ alternate

**3** How would you split the word "gatherers" into syllables?
- ○ gath-er-ers
- ○ gather-ers
- ○ ga-ther-ers
- ○ ga-the-rers

**4** What part of speech is the word "divided" in the following sentence?

The tribes of America could be **divided** into four groups: the hunters, the gatherers, the fishermen, and the farmers.
- ○ noun
- ○ adjective
- ○ adverb
- ○ verb

**5** Which word would finish this analogy?

**Yurok** are to **fishermen** like **Cheyenne** are to _____.
- ○ gatherers
- ○ farmers
- ○ fishermen
- ○ hunters

**6** Which word best completes the following sentence?

The Native American tribes relied on the resources in _____ environments for survival.
- ○ their
- ○ there
- ○ they're
- ○ theirs

Name _____    Date _____

# Get Logical

There are four fourth-grade classrooms at Olson Elementary School. Each class researched a different group of Native American tribes. They will share their reports with the other classes. Use the clues below to decide which group of tribes each class researched.

## Clues

**1** The students in Room 9 did not read about any tribes who lived on the grasslands or the Pacific Northwest Coast.

**2** The gatherers were not researched by an even-numbered classroom.

**3** The students in Room 11 learned about the Cherokee and the Hopi.

**4** The students in Room 10 did not learn about the tribes who used bison skin for clothing and bones for tools.

|  | Room 8 | Room 9 | Room 10 | Room 11 |
|---|---|---|---|---|
| Fishermen |  |  |  |  |
| Farmers |  |  |  |  |
| Gatherers |  |  |  |  |
| Hunters |  |  |  |  |

Room 8 researched _____.

Room 9 researched _____.

Room 10 researched _____.

Room 11 researched _____.

*Integrating Growth of a Nation with Reading Instruction © 2002 Creative Teaching Press*

# Native Tribes Category Sort

## Purpose

The purpose of this activity is for students to use their organization and problem-solving skills to determine and categorize which attributes belong to certain Native American groups.

**MATERIALS**
- ✔ Category Sort Pieces reproducible (page 18)
- ✔ Native Tribes Category Sort (page 19)
- ✔ scissors
- ✔ glue

## Implementation

Give each student a Category Sort Pieces reproducible and a Native Tribes Category Sort. Divide the class into pairs of students. Explain to students that they will work with a partner to sort which characteristics belong to which group of Native Americans. Have students cut out the pieces that list attributes of each group from their category sort page. Then, invite students to glue each group label (i.e., Gatherers, Hunters, Farmers, and Fishermen) in a box across the top of their Native Tribes Category Sort. Challenge students to place each attribute piece under the correct group heading. Discuss the correct answers with the whole class. Tell students to rearrange their pieces if they have any incorrect responses. Then, have students glue each piece in place. As an extension, have each student write a short story or poem in first person as if he or she were a member of one of the tribes. Ask students to include as much detail as possible as they describe where they live, what they do, and what they eat.

### Answer Key

**Gatherers**—were from four different areas; collected camas roots; collected acorns; hunted deer and wild goat; built wickiups with bark, grass, or reeds

**Hunters**—used bison skin for clothing; lived in tipis; used bones to make tools and decorations; lived on grasslands; used horses for hunting

**Farmers**—main food was maize; wove baskets; made pottery with clay; planted beans and squash; made homes from rock, clay, and brush

**Fishermen**—lived in multifamily homes; carved masks and canoes; ate salmon; built cedar plank homes; designed totem poles

*Integrating Growth of a Nation with Reading Instruction © 2002 Creative Teaching Press*

# Category Sort Pieces

| GATHERERS | HUNTERS | FARMERS |
|---|---|---|
| FISHERMEN | were from four different areas | used bison skin for clothing |
| collected camas roots | used horses for hunting | lived in tipis |
| lived on grasslands | collected acorns | lived in multifamily homes |
| hunted deer and wild goat | main food was maize | made homes from rock, clay, and brush |
| ate salmon | built cedar plank homes | built wickiups with bark, grass, or reeds |
| used bones to make tools and decorations | designed totem poles | planted beans and squash |
| made pottery with clay | wove baskets | carved masks and canoes |

*Integrating Growth of a Nation with Reading Instruction © 2002 Creative Teaching Press*

# Native Tribes Category Sort

| Native Group | Native Group | Native Group | Native Group |
|---|---|---|---|
| | | | |
| | | | |
| | | | |

# Catch a Clue

American heroes

Gold Rush

missions

discovery of America

## Our Clues

**1** We will go back in time to the 1500s through 1800s.

**2** We will not learn about Christopher Columbus.

**3** We will not learn about any metals.

**4** We will learn about places where some Native Americans lived and learned new skills.

# Concept Map

Facts we already know about **missions,** and the new facts we have learned

Missions

# Word Warm-Up

Which words might you expect to find in a story about **missions?**

| | | |
|---|---|---|
| voyage | Spain | Christians |
| kingdom | cowboys | soldiers |
| candles | escaped | missionaries |
| church | abandoned | building |

# Spanish Missions in America

In 1492, the King and Queen of Spain paid for a sea voyage. They hoped to discover a faster route to the Orient. If they could get goods like silk and tea faster and safer, their kingdom would become even richer. They paid for Christopher Columbus to make his now famous journey. Columbus did not find a new route. Do you know what he found? You are right if you thought he found a new land. He found new people, new animals, and new resources. He claimed this new land for the country of Spain.

Spain was a world power at this time. It was a rich country. It had a great fleet of ships. Spain was a religious country, too. The Roman Catholic Church was important to this country. The Church and country of Spain wanted to expand beyond its borders. It wanted to show other countries that it owned this huge land called North America. But, it did not have enough Spanish citizens to send to the New World. What could they do?

The Church and the leaders of Spain came up with a plan. The Church believed that the Native Americans should become Christians. Spain wanted citizens to live in and protect the new land. The Church offered to send priest missionaries to see that the missions were built. The missions would teach the Native Americans to become Christians and Spanish citizens. The leaders of Spain would help pay for the missions. They would send soldiers to protect the missions. It seemed like a good plan.

Between the 1500s and the 1800s, the Spanish priests started hundreds of missions. These missions were located throughout the southern part of what is now the United States. Mission sites went from California to North Carolina. The priests taught the Native Americans about their religion. They wanted to teach them how to read the Bible. They baptized many of them. Some of the Native Americans wanted to convert. Others did not. They had their own beliefs. Many converted anyway because they felt they had no choice.

Once a mission was completed, it supplied shelter and meals for the people who lived there. The mission taught the Native Americans how to grow crops and raise animals. It also taught them new skills. The Native Americans learned how to weave, make bricks and tile, make candles and soap, and make pottery. Have you ever made any of these items?

The Native Americans learned a lot from the missions. They lost some things, too. They were no longer free to do as they pleased. They were not allowed to have their old beliefs. They had to be Christians. Families could not live with their children. They could not leave the mission without permission. Sometimes, the Native Americans did not understand why they had to do all of these things.

As years passed, the missions began to fail. The Native Americans escaped or fought back. Sometimes, illnesses killed many of the people. Sometimes, enemies of Spain would attack and destroy a mission. Later, a new government took over and sold many of the missions. The new owners did not take care of the missions, so many of them were abandoned. However, some of the mission sites have been restored, so now you can visit them in person. Have you visited a restored mission site?

*Integrating Growth of a Nation with Reading Instruction © 2002 Creative Teaching Press*

# Comprehension Questions

Integrating Growth of a Nation with Reading Instruction © 2002 Creative Teaching Press

## ? Literal Questions

❶ What did the King and Queen of Spain want Columbus to find on his voyage?

❷ What did Christopher Columbus actually find?

❸ What were some things the Native Americans had and learned at the missions?

❹ What did the Native Americans have to give up to live at a mission?

❺ What were some of the ways Native Americans left the missions?

## ? Inferential Questions

❶ Why do you think the missions were created?

❷ How was mission life like working for "room and board"?

❸ Soldiers were sent to protect the missions. Why do you think protection was necessary?

❹ Native Americans could not leave the mission without permission. Do you think this was fair? Why or why not?

❺ Why do you think some of the missions have been restored?

## ? Making Connections

❶ Do you think you would have chosen to live on a mission? Why or why not?

❷ How is your life similar to the life of a Native American living at a mission? Explain your answer with examples.

❸ If you could visit any restored mission in person, which one would you choose? Why?

❹ In your opinion, were the Native Americans helped or hurt by the establishment of the missions? Explain your answer.

Name _____    Date _____

# Sharpen Your Skills

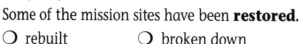

**1** Which word is <u>not</u> a synonym for the word "restored" in the following sentence?

Some of the mission sites have been **restored**.

- ○ rebuilt
- ○ broken down
- ○ refurbished
- ○ renovated

**2** How many syllables are in the word "missionaries"?

- ○ 6
- ○ 4
- ○ 2
- ○ 5

**3** Which word is a comparative adjective in the following sentence?

If you lived on a mission, you may have had to work harder than you do now.

- ○ mission
- ○ may
- ○ harder
- ○ lived

**4** Which word is a synonym for the word "similar" in the following sentence?

Most of the missions in North America had **similar** characteristics.

- ○ common
- ○ different
- ○ unique
- ○ strange

**5** Which word would finish this analogy?

**Missions began** is to the **1500s** like **missions ended** is to the ____ .

- ○ 1700s
- ○ 1900s
- ○ 1800s
- ○ 1600s

**6** Which word best completes the following sentence?

People living at the missions _____ chores and went to school.

- ○ complete
- ○ completed
- ○ completing
- ○ completes

*Integrating Growth of a Nation with Reading Instruction © 2002 Creative Teaching Press*

# Get Logical

Juan Carlos is reading a book about the Spanish missions. It is divided into four chapters with the following titles: "Rules to Follow," "Work to Be Done," "Sacrifices Made," and "Locations." Use the clues below to identify the title of each chapter.

## Clues

❶ The last chapter in Juan Carlos's book explained how the Native Americans living at the missions had to give up their religion and learn how to be good Spanish citizens.

❷ The third chapter did not discuss the work they had to do or the sacrifices they made.

❸ The chapter after "Work to Be Done" included the rules the Native Americans had to follow.

❹ The book began with a map labeled with the name of each mission.

|  | Chapter 1 | Chapter 2 | Chapter 3 | Chapter 4 |
|---|---|---|---|---|
| Rules to Follow |  |  |  |  |
| Work to Be Done |  |  |  |  |
| Sacrifices Made |  |  |  |  |
| Locations |  |  |  |  |

Chapter 1 was titled _____.

Chapter 2 was titled _____.

Chapter 3 was titled _____.

Chapter 4 was titled _____.

# Missions Almanac

## Purpose

The purpose of this activity is for students to learn a variety of facts about different North American missions and about the lives of the people who lived at the missions. They will also practice their research and presentation skills.

> **MATERIALS**
> ✔ Missions Almanac reproducible (page 29)
> ✔ blank paper
> ✔ basket
> ✔ research materials (e.g., Internet, encyclopedias, books)
> ✔ crayons or markers
> ✔ bookbinding materials

San Xavier del Bac
Tucson, Arizona

## Implementation

Explain to students that an almanac is a yearly publication that includes important information such as facts, dates, and statistics about various subjects. Write the names of missions on separate pieces of paper. (Possible missions are listed below.) Each student will need a paper. Fold the papers, put them in a basket, and ask each student to pick one. Give each student a Missions Almanac reproducible. Read aloud and discuss the information students should research. Have students research their mission using encyclopedias, the Internet, and/or books. Encourage students to write information on their reproducible as they read a resource, rather than waiting until after they have completely finished reading. Give each student a piece of paper. Have students draw and color a picture of their mission. Invite each student to present his or her research to the class. Bind together the completed reproducibles and drawings with a cover titled *Missions Almanac for* _____ (insert current school year). Place this book in your reading section for students to reread throughout the school year. Share the almanac created by your class with the students in your class for the next year.

### Possible Mission Sites

| | | |
|---|---|---|
| San Francisco de los Tejas | San Francisco Xavier | La Purísima Concepción de Caborca |
| San Xavier del Bac | Santa Rosalía de Mulegé | Santiago y Nuestra Señora del Pilar de Cocóspera |
| San Juan Capistrano | Santo Domingo | Mission San Ignacio de Cabórica |
| San José | San Pedro Mártir | San Diego de Pitiquito Mission |
| San Esteban Rey de Acoma | San Vincente Ferrar | Mission San José de Tumacacori |
| Nombre de Díos | Santo Tomás | La Purísima Concepcíon de Maria Santisima |
| Nuestra Señora del Carmen | Santa Maria de los Angeles | San Antonio de Oquitoa Mission |
| San Antonio de Valero | San Ignacio | San Pedro y San Pablo de Tubutama |
| Santa Bárbara | San Luis Gonzaga | San Estevan Del Rey Mission |
| Santiago de las Coras | Santa Maria Magdalena | Nuestra Señora de Guadalupe |

*Integrating Growth of a Nation with Reading Instruction © 2002 Creative Teaching Press*

Name _____     Date _____

# Missions Almanac

**Directions:** Read several different research materials to collect information about your mission. As you read, write the information below.

**1** Name of mission:

_____

**2** Location:

_____

**3** Year it was established:

_____

**4** Group of people who lived and worked at this mission:

_____

**5** Population at its busiest time:

_____

**6** Religion that was followed:

_____

**7** Rules that had to be followed:

_____

**8** Describe a day in the life of a Native American living at this mission.

_____

**9** Describe some struggles people had living at this mission.

_____

**10** Date the mission was closed:

_____

**11** Explain why the mission closed.

_____

**12** Can people visit the mission today?

_____

**13** Additional facts about this mission:

_____

Integrating Growth of a Nation with Reading Instruction © 2002 Creative Teaching Press

# Catch a Clue

pioneers

Gold Rush

missions

the first states

Our Clues

**1** We will be learning about the past.

**2** There was a lot of hard work and many high hopes.

**3** It involves people traveling to California.

**4** People expected to become very rich.

*Integrating Growth of a Nation with Reading Instruction © 2002 Creative Teaching Press*

# Concept Map

Facts we already know about the **Gold Rush,** and the new facts we have learned

**The Gold Rush**

# Word Warm-Up

Which words might you expect to find in a story about the **Gold Rush?**

| | | |
|---|---|---|
| metal | treasure | horses |
| president | miners | corrode |
| prospectors | heater | supplies |
| potatoes | government | state |

*Integrating Growth of a Nation with Reading Instruction* © 2002 Creative Teaching Press

# The Gold Rush

Imagine you are standing by the end of a stream. Something catches your eye. It shines in the sun. Curious, you bend down and pick it up. The shiny yellow rock makes you think of one thing—gold! Wouldn't it be exciting to find a lump of gold? That was how James Marshall felt. In January 1848, James Marshall was working at Sutter's Mill outside of Sacramento, California, when a lump of shiny metal in the millrace caught his eye. He banged the lump with a rock. It did not shatter. He placed it in a pot of boiling lye. It did not tarnish. "Maybe this is gold," he thought.

Marshall showed the metal to his boss, Captain Sutter. Captain Sutter put nitric acid on the lump. It did not corrode. Then, he weighed the metal. It was heavier than silver. It was gold! The two men wanted the men at the mill to keep working. They wanted to keep the gold to themselves. But, it was a hard secret to keep. Soon, many other people knew about the discovery.

Tales about treasure are easy to tell. It did not take long for tales about gold in California to become exaggerated. Many people felt that these stories were not true. Many of them were not. Then, President James Polk told Congress that the supply of gold was very large. People thought that what the president said must be true. By 1849, the rush to find gold in California was on. The miners would become known as the forty-niners. This was because most people traveled to the gold fields in 1849.

When the prospectors arrived in California, they needed to buy supplies such as a gold pan, a pick and shovel, food, and a place to stay. Storekeepers were ready to sell miners the things they needed. Towns sprang up overnight so that the miners had a place to lodge. People crowded into the gold fields to stake their claim. They did not care if someone else owned the land. They believed they were going to strike it rich. The prospectors did find gold, but they were not getting rich. Because they spent all of their time looking for gold, they had to buy supplies from other people. The miners began to notice that prices were very high. Eggs cost ten dollars a dozen. Potatoes sold for one dollar each. Laundry service was so expensive that dirty clothes were shipped to China or Hawaii. It was cheaper than paying the local laundries to wash clothes.

Violence and crime became a problem. There were too many people crowded into the gold fields and towns. Some men thought it would be easier to steal gold from others than to mine it on their own. People realized they would need stricter laws and a form of government. The people wrote a constitution and asked for the territory of California to become ratified as a state. California became a state in 1850.

At last the Gold Rush came to an end. Most of the gold that was easy to mine was gone. The only gold left was deep underground or hidden in quartz. Businesses took over the mining of the gold. The days of the lone prospector were over. What happened to James Marshall? He never did strike it rich. He was forced off of his own claim by other miners. He never found any more gold. He died a poor man in 1885. However, he will always be famous for starting the California Gold Rush.

*Integrating Growth of a Nation with Reading Instruction* © 2002 Creative Teaching Press

# Comprehension Questions

## Literal Questions

❶ Who first discovered gold in California? When? Where?

❷ What did Captain Sutter do to the lump to test it for gold?

❸ Who was the president at the time? What did he do?

❹ What happened to James Marshall?

❺ When did California become a state? Why?

## Inferential Questions

❶ How do you think we still are able to get gold today?

❷ What problems did people who traveled to California in search of gold have when they arrived? Do you think this is what they expected? Why or why not?

❸ Why do you think that the Gold Rush led to violence and crime? How would new laws help this problem?

❹ Why do you think prices for goods were raised so high during the Gold Rush?

❺ Why do you think people bought goods at such high prices?

## Making Connections

❶ If you lived in the year 1849 and you heard that you could become rich, would you go try to find some gold? Why or why not?

❷ Do you think that James Marshall and Captain Sutter should have told anyone about their find? Why or why not?

❸ Some of the prospectors were greedy. Has there ever been a time in your life that you were greedy? What did you want? Did you get it? How?

❹ If you were a storekeeper, do you think you would have raised your prices? Why or why not?

# Sharpen Your Skills

**1** Which guide words in the dictionary would help you find the word "prospector"?

- ❍ prior–proper
- ❍ productive–propel
- ❍ prosper–protect
- ❍ proscribe–protein

**2** What kind of sentence is the following sentence?

Wouldn't it be exciting to find a lump of gold?

- ❍ exclamatory
- ❍ declarative
- ❍ interrogative
- ❍ command

**3** If you wanted to find an antonym for the word "greedy," which resource would be the most helpful?

- ❍ encyclopedia
- ❍ dictionary
- ❍ thesaurus
- ❍ almanac

**4** Which word is an adjective in the following sentence?

In January 1848, John Marshall was working at Sutter's Mill when a lump of shiny metal in the millrace caught his eye.

- ❍ shiny
- ❍ working
- ❍ caught
- ❍ eye

**5** Which word would finish this analogy?

**Farmer** is to **eggs** like _____ is to **gold.**

- ❍ surveyor
- ❍ collector
- ❍ chef
- ❍ prospector

**6** Which word best completes the following sentence?

The lucky discovery of gold _____ many people to the state of California.

- ❍ laid
- ❍ lead
- ❍ led
- ❍ lad

*Integrating Growth of a Nation with Reading Instruction © 2002 Creative Teaching Press*

Name _____  Date _____

Courtney checked out a library book called *The California Gold Rush*. It had four main chapters. Use the clues below to identify the title of each chapter.

## Clues

❶ The first and second chapters did not have any information on the problems that the prospectors were dealing with at the time.

❷ The first chapter discussed a person involved with first discovering gold in California.

❸ The year when many miners rushed to find gold in California was not discussed in an odd-numbered chapter.

❹ Neither chapter 2 nor chapter 3 discussed the era after California became a state.

|  | Chapter 1 | Chapter 2 | Chapter 3 | Chapter 4 |
|---|---|---|---|---|
| Later Years |  |  |  |  |
| Hardships |  |  |  |  |
| 1849 |  |  |  |  |
| James Marshall |  |  |  |  |

Chapter 1 was titled _____.

Chapter 2 was titled _____.

Chapter 3 was titled _____.

Chapter 4 was titled _____.

# Potential Prospector

## Purpose

The purpose of this activity is to have students practice persuasive writing while thinking about what gold prospectors would have to go through to strike it rich. It will also give them an opportunity to experience panning for gold themselves!

### MATERIALS

- ✔ Persuasive Writing Frame reproducible (page 39)
- ✔ Potential Prospector reproducible (page 40)
- ✔ small rocks and pebbles
- ✔ gold spray paint
- ✔ small plastic pool or large flat bucket
- ✔ water
- ✔ pie tins

## Implementation

In advance, collect some small rocks and pebbles, and spray-paint them gold. Fill a small plastic pool or large flat bucket with water. Place the gold rocks and pebbles in the water. Explain to students that they will write a persuasive letter as if they lived back in 1849 to convince you that they would make great prospectors for gold. If they do convince you, they will get to pan for gold! Review the important aspects of a persuasive letter. Explain to students the importance of beginning with an attention-grabber such as a question, quote, or humorous statement to catch the reader's attention; stating their reasons; and providing backup information that explains the benefit of that reason. For example a student could write *I would make a super prospector because I am strong. This is a benefit because the traveling is long and treacherous. A strong person will survive it much better.* Remind students to conclude their letters with a final statement that restates their opinion and most important points. Give each student a Persuasive Writing Frame reproducible. Ask students to brainstorm some reasons why they think they would make a great prospector and the benefits of those reasons and write the ideas on their paper. Then, give each student a Potential Prospector reproducible. Have students use their brainstorming notes to write a persuasive letter to you. Encourage volunteers to read their letter to the class. Have the class vote for whose letter was the most persuasive. Then, have each student use a pie tin to pan for "gold."

# Persuasive Writing Frame

Topic sentence: _____

Reason #1: _____

Benefit: _____

Reason #2: _____

Benefit: _____

Reason #3: _____

Benefit: _____

# Potential Prospector

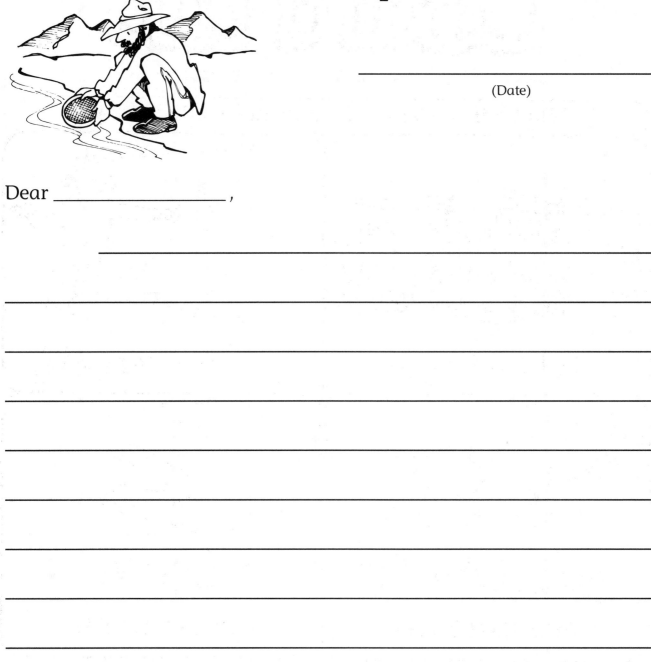

_____
(Date)

Dear _____ ,

_____

_____

_____

_____

_____

_____

_____

_____

_____

Sincerely,

_____
(Signature)

*Integrating Growth of a Nation with Reading Instruction © 2002 Creative Teaching Press*

# Catch a Clue

## What will we learn about in our reading today?

White House

teachers

sea animals

government

**Our Clues**

1. We will talk about responsibilities.

2. It involves taking charge.

3. It involves your city, state, and country.

4. It could be a part of your classroom.

# Concept Map

Facts we already know about the **branches of government,** and the new facts we have learned

Branches of
Government

*Integrating Growth of a Nation with Reading Instruction* © 2002 Creative Teaching Press

# Word Warm-Up

Which words might you expect to find in a story about the **branches of government?**

| | | |
|---|---|---|
| colonies | Constitution | judge |
| England | senators | president |
| money | apartment | veto |
| checks | bill | business |

# Branches of Government

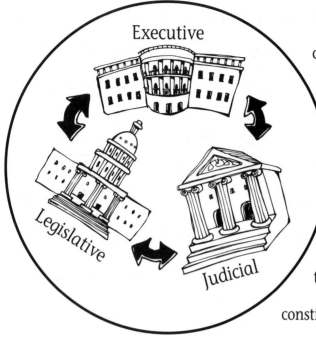

Executive

Legislative

Judicial

The colonies in America fought a war to become a country. They fought against the King of England. They felt the King did not care about their needs and that he had too much power.

Do you like when people listen to your ideas? Have you ever thought a rule was unfair and wanted to change it? Well, the first citizens of the United States felt like this. They decided to write a constitution to be heard and to change some rules. This constitution set up a national government. This government would listen to what the people wanted. The writers did such a good job that this government still works today. The Constitution stated that the federal government could do certain things. It could collect taxes. It could create money. It could declare war and provide for the defense of the nation. It could control how business was done. The Constitution also set up three branches of the government. They are the executive, the legislative, and the judicial branches.

Why are there three branches? The writers of the Constitution did not want any one part of the government to become too powerful. The Constitution set up a system of checks and balances. Each branch could check what the others were doing. Each branch could balance out the actions of another.

The legislative branch is sometimes called Congress. It is split into two parts: the Senate and the House of Representatives. The Senate has 100 members. They are called senators. Each state gets to elect two senators. They serve a six-year term. The House of Representatives has 435 members. They are called representatives. Each state elects a number of representatives based on how many people live in

*Integrating Growth of a Nation with Reading Instruction © 2002 Creative Teaching Press*

the state. Do you know how many people live in your state? A representative serves a two-year term. The main job of the legislative branch is to make laws. This starts with the idea of a bill. A bill is like the first draft of a law. About 10,000 bills are given to Congress each year. Only about 650 of those bills become laws. What do you think happens to the rest of them?

The executive branch includes the president and the committees that serve under the president. He makes rules based on the laws. He makes sure the rules and laws are followed. He decides how money is spent. He is the head of our country. The president is elected for a four-year term. He can serve no more than two terms. He must approve the laws voted on by Congress before they can become laws. The president can veto, or say "no" to, laws that he does not like just like your parents can "veto" watching a movie on a school night.

The judicial branch is made up of the Supreme Court and its judges. The Supreme Court is the highest court in the nation. The Supreme Court decides what the laws mean. Supreme Court judges are elected for life. Sometimes a judge may decide to retire. When there is an opening, the president appoints a new judge. Congress needs to approve this person. Then, the new judge can take office.

How does each branch check and balance the others? The president can veto any law created by Congress. Congress can revote on a law that the president vetoes. The Supreme Court can decide that a law is unconstitutional. Each branch can watch what the other branch is doing. If a branch is abusing its power, the other two can take action against it. This keeps them balanced and fair.

The writers of our Constitution did a fine job. They were wise to set up three branches of government. They made sure that it is a government of the people, by the people, and for the people of the United States.

# Comprehension Questions

*Integrating Growth of a Nation with Reading Instruction* © 2002 Creative Teaching Press

**?** ## Literal Questions

1. Who did the colonies fight a war against to become a country?

2. List at least three things the Constitution stated that the federal government could do.

3. What are the three branches of government?

4. What is the main job of the executive, legislative, and judicial branches?

5. How long is the term that a Supreme Court judge serves?

 ## Inferential Questions

1. Which branch of government do you think is related to a judge and jury? Why?

2. Why do you think different states have different laws when they are in the same country?

3. How do you think life would be different without any form of government? Explain your answer.

4. Why do you think Congress can revote on a law that the president vetoes?

5. Why do you think senators, presidents, and representatives can only serve a certain number of terms in the same position?

 ## Making Connections

1. If you were going to do a report on one branch of the federal government, which would be the most interesting to you? Why?

2. Research three laws that your state government has passed.

3. If your classroom were set up like our government, who would be considered the president?

4. Research how many people live in your state and how many representatives your state has based on this number.

Name _____    Date _____

# Sharpen Your Skills

**1** How would you split the word "judicial" into syllables?

- ○ ju-di-cial
- ○ ju-dic-ial
- ○ j-u-d-i-cial
- ○ jud-i-cial

**2** Which sentence below states an opinion—not a fact?

- ○ The legislative branch is the most important.
- ○ The executive branch includes the president.
- ○ The judicial branch includes the Supreme Court and its judges.
- ○ The legislative branch is in charge of making laws.

**3** What would be the best synonym for the word "declare" in the following sentence?

This branch could **declare** war and provide for the defense of the nation.

- ○ conceal
- ○ supply
- ○ announce
- ○ cover

**4** What part of speech is the word "stated" in the following sentence?

The Constitution **stated** that the federal government could do certain things.

- ○ conjunction
- ○ proper noun
- ○ adjective
- ○ verb

**5** Which word would finish this analogy?

**Legislative branch** is to **Congress** like **judicial branch** is to

_____ .

- ○ laws
- ○ Supreme Court
- ○ representatives
- ○ senators

**6** Which word best completes the following sentence?

It is your _____ to obey all local, state, and federal laws.

- ○ responsibility
- ○ response
- ○ meaning
- ○ choices

Integrating Growth of a Nation with Reading Instruction © 2002 Creative Teaching Press

Name _____     Date _____

Carrie, Brenton, Phillip, and Marsha each have one parent who has a government job. Use the clues below to decide the job title of each student's parent.

**Clues**

**1** Marsha's mom works for the state of Washington and has served three years of her six-year term.

**2** Brenton's dad is not in charge of listening to lawyers defend people to decide if they are guilty or innocent.

**3** Carrie's dad does not work for Congress.

**4** Phillip's mom works in one part of the Congress and will serve a two-year term.

|  | Carrie | Brenton | Phillip | Marsha |
|---|---|---|---|---|
| Judge |  |  |  |  |
| Representative |  |  |  |  |
| Senator |  |  |  |  |
| President |  |  |  |  |

Carrie's parent is a _____.

Brenton's parent is a _____.

Phillip's parent is a _____.

Marsha's parent is a _____.

*Integrating Growth of a Nation with Reading Instruction © 2002 Creative Teaching Press*

# Name That Branch

## Purpose

The purpose of this activity is for students to practice identifying the responsibilities of each branch of government in America.

## Implementation

Give each student three index cards. Have students label their cards *legislative branch, judicial branch,* and *executive branch.* Read aloud a clue from the Name That Branch Clue Cards. Allow a short period of time for students to think of the corresponding branch of government. Then, say *Show me!* Have students raise the card with their answer. For example, say *This branch includes the Senate.* Students should hold up their legislative branch card. After all students have shown their answer card, tell them the correct answer, and discuss why it is correct. Repeat these steps with each clue. As an extension activity, give each child a set of Name That Branch Clue Cards and a Name That Branch Category Sort. Ask students to cut apart the clue cards and then place each card under the correct heading on the category sort. When students have correctly placed the cards, have them glue each card to the page.

### Answer Key

**Legislative**—gives passed bills to the president to approve; includes the House of Representatives; includes the Senate; includes Congress; has the right to make laws; writes, debates, and passes bills; includes the congressmen and congresswomen who are elected for a term of two years

**Executive**—includes the president; includes the vice president; includes committees that serve under the president; makes sure that the laws are followed; the president heads this branch; decides how money is spent

**Judicial**—includes the Supreme Court; includes a position for a person who is elected for life; includes the court system; settles arguments related to the meaning of laws; includes the highest court in the nation

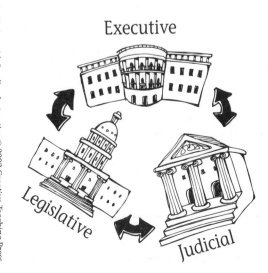

Executive

Legislative

Judicial

# Name That Branch Clue Cards

| | | |
|---|---|---|
| Gives passed bills to the president to approve | Includes the Supreme Court | Includes the House of Representatives |
| Includes the Senate | Includes the president | Includes the vice president |
| Includes Congress | Includes committees that serve under the president | Has the right to make laws |
| Includes a position for a person who is elected for life | Writes, debates, and passes bills | Makes sure that the laws are followed |
| Includes the court system | Settles arguments related to the meaning of laws | Includes the congressmen and congresswomen who are elected for a term of two years |
| The president heads this branch | Includes the highest court in the nation | Decides how money is spent |

*Integrating Growth of a Nation with Reading Instruction © 2002 Creative Teaching Press*

Name _____     Date _____

# Name That Branch Category Sort

| Executive Branch | Legislative Branch | Judicial Branch |
| --- | --- | --- |
|  |  |  |
|  |  |  |
|  |  |  |
|  |  |  |
|  |  |  |
|  |  |  |

# Catch a Clue

**What will we learn about in our reading today?**

historical documents

Congress

Abraham Lincoln    John F. Kennedy

U.S. presidents

how the railroads began

## Our Clues

**1** It is related to our past.

**2** The topic is not related to transportation.

**3** We will learn how a nation was formed.

**4** We will not focus on the leaders of our country.

# Concept Map

Facts we already know about **historical documents,** and the new facts we have learned

**Historical Documents**

# Word Warm-Up

Which words might you expect to find in a story about **historical documents?**

| | | |
|---|---|---|
| Washington, D.C. | statues | Constitution |
| colonies | King | national |
| government | branches | foundation |
| amendments | suitcase | bald eagle |

*Integrating Growth of a Nation with Reading Instruction © 2002 Creative Teaching Press*

# Historical Documents

During summer vacation, I went to Washington, D.C. with my dad. We saw the Washington Monument and the Lincoln Memorial, and we read some of the names on the Vietnam Veterans Memorial. Then, my dad showed me something very special. We climbed a set of steps and went into a stone building. People were looking at something in a glass case. We saw that they were looking at the original Declaration of Independence. Next to it, I could see the original Constitution and the Bill of Rights for the United States.

A tour guide told us that the Declaration of Independence, the Constitution, and the Bill of Rights are historical documents. This means that they are pieces of paper that are important to a country's history. These three documents are key because they helped to form a new nation—the United States of America.

The Declaration of Independence was written because of the way that England was treating the colonies. At that time, there were thirteen colonies. These colonies were a part of England. They thought England was abusing their rights. The colonists thought that a committee should write a paper that declared their independence from England. Thomas Jefferson was asked to write the first draft. The committee members looked it over, made some changes, and on July 4, 1776, Congress agreed to the final draft. It became the Declaration of Independence.

What was so vital about the Declaration of Independence? This document said that some-

Integrating Growth of a Nation with Reading Instruction © 2002 Creative Teaching Press

times it was necessary to get rid of a bad government. It said that people could have certain rights. It gave examples of how badly King George III had been treating the colonies. Most importantly, it declared that the colonies were no longer a part of England. The colonies were now a separate country. It was called the United States of America. Now, they could make their own rules.

The Constitution is another important historical document. After the colonists declared independence, people saw that the states were not acting like one country. They were acting like thirteen separate countries. George Washington and other leaders thought that if they formed a new national government, the states would start working together. To do this, people from each state came together for many meetings to discuss new laws. They wrote these new laws in a document called the Constitution. Congress accepted the Constitution on September 17, 1787. The Constitution is sometimes called the "supreme law of the land." This is because it states the laws that the country must follow. It tells how the government should work. It sets up three branches of government. Sometimes in history, it is decided that the Constitution is missing an important law. Therefore, changes or additions are made to the Constitution. These new laws are called amendments.

The Bill of Rights is important because it promises certain rights for United States citizens. It grants freedom of speech, the right to choose whatever religion people want to practice, and the right to a fair and quick trial. It allows people the right to get together as a group and talk about anything they want. These rights were important to the colonists. Not all countries have these rights. The colonists wanted to make sure that the citizens of the United States had them.

After our trip, I thought a lot about the rights and freedoms I have as a citizen of the United States and how these historical documents are the foundation of America. I am thankful that the founders of my country created these documents.

*Integrating Growth of a Nation with Reading Instruction © 2002 Creative Teaching Press*

# Comprehension Questions

## Literal Questions

1. What is a historical document?

2. Which three historical documents did you read about?

3. Which document is sometimes called the "supreme law of the land"?

4. Which document was created out of Americans' desire to be independent from British rule?

5. Which historical document lists your rights as an American citizen?

## Inferential Questions

1. Why is each historical document important? Explain your answer in detail.

2. How would life in America be different if the Bill of Rights did not exist?

3. Why was the Declaration of Independence so important to the nation?

4. If you could travel back in time, would you want to be British or a member of one of the original colonies? Why?

5. Why was Thomas Jefferson such an important person?

## Making Connections

1. If you could add or delete one item from the Bill of Rights, what would it be? Explain your answer.

2. How would your life have been different if you were born fifty years before the Declaration of Independence? Why? Would you want to live in that time period? Why or why not?

3. What would you ask Thomas Jefferson if you could travel back in time and have lunch with him?

4. Which historical document affects your life the most today? Explain your answer.

# Sharpen Your Skills

**1** Which guide words in the dictionary would help you find the word "independence"?

- ○ indulgence–industry
- ○ incriminate–indirect
- ○ inappropriate–increase
- ○ index–induct

**2** Look at these words: independent–indivisible–indestructible.

What is the meaning of the prefix "in"?

- ○ three
- ○ bad
- ○ across
- ○ not

**3** If you wanted to learn more about the details of the Declaration of Independence, which resource would be the most helpful?

- ○ encyclopedia
- ○ thesaurus
- ○ dictionary
- ○ almanac

**4** What is the root word in the word "declaration"?

- ○ declarative
- ○ declare
- ○ declaring
- ○ clare

**5** Which word or phrase would finish this analogy?

**Bill of Rights** is to **a person's rights** like _____ is to **a country's law.**

- ○ Thomas Jefferson
- ○ Washington Monument
- ○ Declaration of Independence
- ○ Constitution of the United States

**6** Which word best completes the following sentence?

Thomas Jefferson _____ the first version of the Declaration of Independence.

- ○ draft
- ○ drafter
- ○ drafts
- ○ drafted

*Integrating Growth of a Nation with Reading Instruction © 2002 Creative Teaching Press*

Mr. Colby's class is breaking off into four groups to research an aspect of some historical documents. The groups will be color-coded. Use the clues below to decide which area each group researched.

## Clues

**1** The purple group learned about the person who wrote the first draft of the Declaration of Independence.

**2** The blue group did not learn more about the British rule.

**3** The red group did not learn about how the national government in America was formed. Neither did the blue group.

**4** The group that researched various rights for citizens of the United States was not the color of the sky.

| | Blue | Green | Purple | Red |
|---|---|---|---|---|
| Declaration of Independence | | | | |
| Bill of Rights | | | | |
| United States Constitution | | | | |
| Thomas Jefferson | | | | |

The blue group researched _____.

The green group researched _____.

The purple group researched _____.

The red group researched _____.

# Classroom Bill of Rights

## Purpose

The purpose of this activity is for students to gain a greater understanding of how the Bill of Rights was created. Students will also practice their presentation skills and working cooperatively in a group.

### MATERIALS

✔ Classroom Bill of Rights reproducible (page 61)
✔ glue
✔ light-colored construction paper
✔ markers

## Implementation

Discuss with students the types of ideas that are in the Bill of Rights (e.g., freedom of religion and speech, end of slavery, women's right to vote). Explain that these amendments were written to add personal guarantees to the people of the United States that the original Constitution did not include. Tell students that the Bill of Rights describes the fundamental liberties of Americans that cannot be taken away by the government. Tell students they will be creating a Classroom Bill of Rights that cannot be taken away by the teacher. Divide the class into groups of four to five students. Give each group a Classroom Bill of Rights reproducible. Invite groups to brainstorm five "amendments" they think would be valuable to include in a Classroom Bill of Rights. Ask students to write their ideas and reasoning on the reproducible. Remind students that the five amendments need to be agreed upon by the whole group. Invite groups to present their ideas and reasons to the class. Write the proposed amendments on the chalkboard. Then, have the class vote on each amendment. The five amendments that receive the most votes will become the Classroom Bill of Rights. (The teacher has the final vote, of course.) Write the final five amendments on a new reproducible, and glue it in the center of a large piece of light-colored construction paper. Invite each student to use a marker to sign his or her name on the construction paper around the reproducible. Post the paper next to your current set of classroom rules.

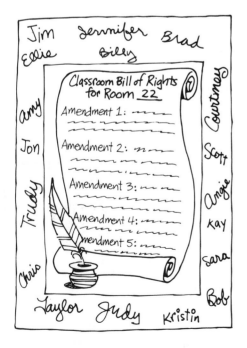

*Integrating Growth of a Nation with Reading Instruction © 2002 Creative Teaching Press*

# Classroom Bill of Rights
## for Room _____

**Amendment 1:**

_____

_____

_____

**Amendment 2:**

_____

_____

_____

**Amendment 3:**

_____

_____

_____

**Amendment 4:**

_____

_____

_____

**Amendment 5:**

_____

_____

_____

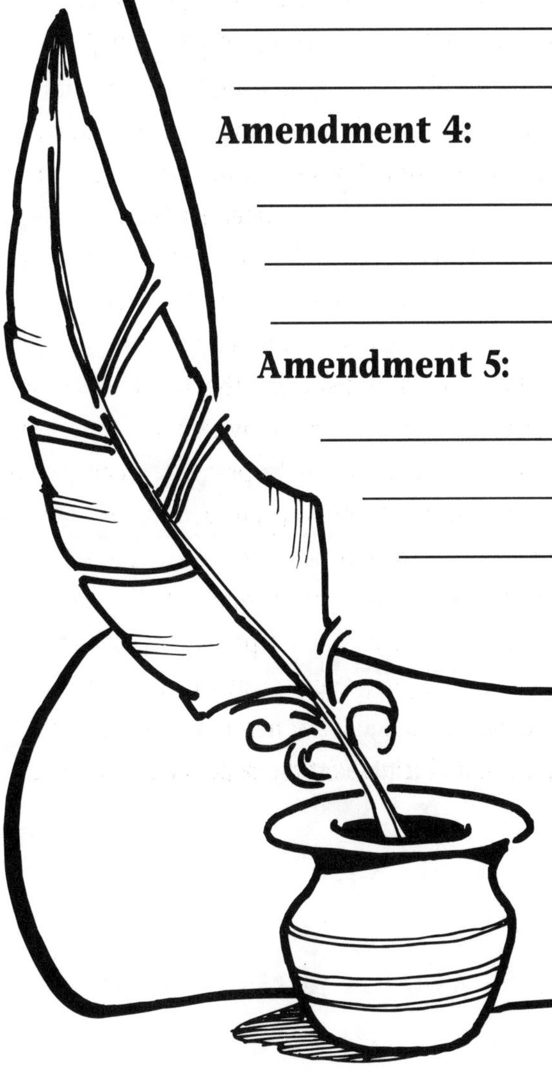

# Catch a Clue

laws

citizens

heroes

milk shakes

## Our Clues

**1** They are in your city, state, and country.

**2** They are men, women, and students.

**3** We will discuss rights people have.

**4** We will focus on people who are part of a country.

*Integrating Growth of a Nation with Reading Instruction* © 2002 Creative Teaching Press

# Concept Map

Facts we already know about **citizenship**, and the new facts we have learned

Citizenship

# Word Warm-Up

Which words might you expect to find in a story about **citizenship?**

| | | |
|---|---|---|
| ceremony | country | naturalization |
| religion | assembly | register |
| speech | overthrow | loyalty |
| school | expatriation | volunteer |

*Integrating Growth of a Nation with Reading Instruction © 2002 Creative Teaching Press*

# Citizenship

SooJoon is excited. Today is September 17th. It is Citizenship Day. Today, SooJoon and her family will be a part of a special ceremony. They will pledge their loyalty to America and become citizens. What does it mean to be a citizen? Citizenship is when a person is a full member of a nation. Sometimes we call it nationality. Each country has its own rules to be a citizen. In the United States, a citizen has certain rights and duties. The most basic of these rights are called civil rights. One of these rights is the freedom of speech. It means people can say their own opinions. The freedom to choose any religion is also a right. People can worship as they choose without being bothered. They have the right to assembly. This means people can gather with any group they want. People have the right to vote for the members of their government. In this way, they choose who best stands for what they want. People have the right to run for office themselves.

There are limits to some of these rights. A citizen must be at least eighteen years old to vote. Some states ask that citizens register before they can vote. They cannot tell lies about people to damage their name and who they are. We cannot yell "Fire!" in a place when there is not a fire. As citizens of the United States, people have the right to travel throughout it. They cannot be forced to leave the country. They cannot have their citizenship taken away without a reason.

Citizens also have civic duties. The law calls for these civic duties. Citizens of the United States must pay taxes. They might be asked to guard their country. If a person is called, he or she

Integrating Growth of a Nation with Reading Instruction © 2002 Creative Teaching Press

should serve on a jury for a trial. Other duties are not laws, but they help a person to be a better citizen. For example, it is important to read and think about issues that affect the country. We should also help others, and we should vote.

How does a person become a citizen? The most common way is by being born in a country. In this way, a person is a citizen by birth. SooJoon and her family are becoming citizens. They were citizens of another country. Naturalization is the way foreigners can become U.S. citizens. SooJoon and her family will become naturalized citizens. When people become citizens of the U.S., there are some rules they must follow. They have to live in the U.S. for a number of years. In most cases, they must give up their citizenship of any other country. They also have to pledge their loyalty to the United States.

Can citizens of the U.S. lose their citizenship? The answer is yes. Some may choose to give up their citizenship. This is called expatriation. For some serious actions, citizenship can be taken away. People who become citizens of another country will lose their citizenship. People who try to overthrow the government by force will lose their citizenship. People can also lose their citizenship if they serve in another country's armed forces.

SooJoon is proud that she will be a part of the United States of America. She will follow all of the laws. She will follow the laws to be the best citizen she can be and to help make the United States a great country.

Integrating Growth of a Nation with Reading Instruction © 2002 Creative Teaching Press

# Comprehension Questions

Integrating Growth of a Nation with Reading Instruction © 2002 Creative Teaching Press

## Literal Questions

❶ What is a citizen?

❷ What are some duties a citizen of the United States <u>must</u> do? What are some duties someone could do just to be a better citizen?

❸ Name some limits to the rights of American citizens.

❹ What does the United States guarantee to citizens of its country?

❺ Can a citizen of the United States lose his or her citizenship? How?

## Inferential Questions

❶ Why do you think a person has to meet many requirements before he or she becomes a citizen of the United States?

❷ Why do you think people cannot yell "Fire!" when there is not a fire?

❸ How do you think completing jury duty might make you a better citizen?

❹ Do you know someone who has completed a civic duty? What did he or she do?

❺ Why is it important to read and learn about issues that affect your country?

## Making Connections

❶ What rights do you have now? What additional rights will you have as you grow older?

❷ What are some civic duties that you might be able to do right now? What are some civic duties you would like to do when you are older?

❸ How did you become a citizen of your country?

❹ If you had to pick just one civil right (e.g., freedom of speech, freedom of religion) to keep, which one would you pick? Why?

# Sharpen Your Skills

**1** If you wanted to know how to divide the word "citizenship" into syllables, which resource would be the most helpful?

○ encyclopedia    ○ dictionary

○ thesaurus    ○ atlas

**2** What part of the word "enforcement" is "ment"?

Police officers are in charge of **enforcement** of the laws.

○ prefix    ○ suffix

○ word    ○ root

**3** What does the word "member" mean in the following sentence?

Citizenship is when a person is a full **member** of a nation.

○ separation    ○ speaker

○ class    ○ part of

**4** What part of speech is the word "great" in the following sentences?

You should always treat others the way you want to be treated.

That is the first step in becoming a **great** citizen.

○ adjective    ○ pronoun

○ adverb    ○ conjunction

**5** Which phrase would finish this analogy?

**The freedom of speech** is to **civil rights** like ____ is to **civic duty.**

○ serving on a jury    ○ saying the Pledge of Allegiance

○ joining a religion    ○ becoming the President of the U.S.

**6** Which of the following statements is a fragment—not a sentence?

○ Be kind to others.

○ Being a good citizen.

○ Senior citizens deserve respect.

○ You are a citizen right now.

*Integrating Growth of a Nation with Reading Instruction © 2002 Creative Teaching Press*

Name _____     Date _____

Each of SooJoon's family members was looking forward to a particular part of becoming a citizen of the United States. Use the clues below to decide which aspect of becoming a citizen each family member was excited about.

## Clues

1. SooJoon's father could not wait to visit each state within the United States!

2. The person ready to continue telling lots of people that "Animals Have Rights, Too!" is not SooJoon's mother.

3. The person who is excited to vote and who would someday like to serve on a jury is not SooJoon or her brother.

4. SooJoon gets nervous speaking in front of large groups, but is excited to pledge her loyalty to America.

| | SooJoon | SooJoon's Father | SooJoon's Mother | SooJoon's Brother |
|---|---|---|---|---|
| The Pledge of Allegiance | | | | |
| Freedom of Speech | | | | |
| Civil Rights | | | | |
| Citizens' Duties | | | | |

SooJoon is excited about _____.

SooJoon's father is excited about _____.

SooJoon's mother is excited about _____.

SooJoon's brother is excited about _____.

Integrating Growth of a Nation with Reading Instruction © 2002 Creative Teaching Press

# Becoming a Citizen

## Purpose

The purpose of this activity is for students to gain an understanding about how a person becomes a citizen of the United States. Students will also practice their interviewing and presentation skills.

### MATERIALS

- ✔ Becoming a Citizen reproducible (page 71)
- ✔ Thank You! reproducible (page 72)
- ✔ crayons or markers

## Implementation

Prior to having students complete this activity, send home a parent letter to explain it. Ask parents to help their child choose a person to interview. Explain that the interviews can take place in person or over the phone. Explain to students that they will interview a person who came to America from another country to find out the process he or she needed to go through to become a citizen. Give each student a Becoming a Citizen reproducible. Read aloud and discuss the questions on the reproducible. Allow students a week or two to complete the interview. Have students present their information to the class. Then, discuss with them the new information they have learned. If a student is unable to find a person to interview, have him or her research the questions using the encyclopedia or the Internet. The student can write down information that applies to all people who want to become citizens. When students have completed this activity, have them use the Thank You! reproducible to write a thank-you letter to the person they interviewed. Invite students to color the border of the letter. This letter will show respect for that person, as well as give students an opportunity to be good citizens. If a student completed the research instead of the interview, have him or her write a letter to you explaining what he or she learned.

*Integrating Growth of a Nation with Reading Instruction © 2002 Creative Teaching Press*

Name _____  Date _____

# Becoming a Citizen

**The person I interviewed is:** _____

In school, I am learning about how a person becomes a citizen of a country.
I would like to ask you some questions about how you became a citizen of this country.

**1** What country did you move from? _____

**2** Why did you choose to leave that country? _____

**3** When did you come to this country? _____

**4** How did you come to this country? _____

**5** How long did you have to be in this country before you became a citizen? _____

**6** Did you have to take any classes or tests? _____ If so, what were they? _____

_____

**7** What other things did you have to do to become a citizen of this country? _____

_____

**8** Did you speak the language of this country when you came? _____ If not, how did you
learn it?_____

**9** Were you able to work or go to school when you came to this country? _____ What did
you have to do before you could?_____

**10** What was the most difficult part of becoming a citizen? _____

**11** What is your most memorable experience of becoming a citizen?_____

_____

**12** Do you have different rights in this country than the country you came from? _____
What are some of them?_____

**13** What is the biggest difference between the two countries?_____

**14** Is there any part of the country you came from that you miss? _____ If so, what is it?

_____

**15** Are you glad you came to this country? _____ Why or why not? _____

**Thank you for sharing your experience with me!**

# Thank You!

_____

(Date)

**Dear** _____ ,

_____

_____

_____

_____

_____

_____

_____

_____

_____

_____

**Sincerely,**

_____

_Integrating Growth of a Nation with Reading Instruction © 2002 Creative Teaching Press_